Private
People

Self Portraits

Edited by
John Jones

The Collective Press

© The Collective Press 1999

Cover design
& Layout ©

Cataloguing In Publication Data for this book is available
from the British Library

ISBN 1 899449 50 7

Published with the financial support of the
Arts Council of Wales.

Front cover;
Original drawing by Aneirin Jones *(a self portrait at 3½ years)*

Quote - intro; Richard Chenevix Trench.

Printed in Great Britain by Redwood Books

Main Typeface; Futura Md BT 11pt.

Preface

I have often waited to name a new born foal, as if the name itself was a wind blown thing and would only settle when the time was right.

Here is a book that was, for a long time, an idea, blown about and hard to settle. The names it holds are those who willingly used both time and talent to support The Collective's work; those who promoted poetry and on the way, helped some *'new writers'* achieve recognition in a commercially hostile environment.

This book is an invitation to you, its reader, to study and appreciate the 'Private People' it contains; and it does contain a diverse collection of poetry talent. From ranters to surrealists, academics to graffiti artists, some more in tune with the disaffected and the waste land than with those that haunt the bookshelf. We are here to make the question, "Do you like poetry?" as relevant as "Do you like music?" The answer would be "Yes", the only other question, "Which type?"

I have had the good fortune to have met all the poets who contributed to this book. I have read with most of them. They have shown me that 'individual art' requires its own truth. To achieve this, the very least one needs is belief, even if that belief is only in the 'art' itself. Unfortunately for some, it was, and may still be, the only positive thing left in their life.

In my work on the land I have seen many living things stunted and deformed from the harsh realities that exist there. Some of the survivors are tough, hard-nosed little bastards that I find I admire greatly. Art forms, such as poetry, and public bodies that support them, similarly face tough times, unable to flourish when neglected or under-funded by the society they stem from. Yes, the artist will survive, long enough at least to say something, he always does; but what treasures are lost when the living's too hard? If art is a nation's soul, we starve it at our peril. Continue and we will, if we haven't already done so, breed a tough, hard-nosed, bastard of a society, which for some reason we won't admire at all.

We thank you for purchasing this book and in doing so backing an art form, long cherished but often undernourished. Your support is valued.

John Jones

Contents

Contributors

Contents

Contributors

*He did not thus
begin the world with names
but with the power of naming.*

(and i am *taurus*:
minotaur unwanted /
guarded/
slaughtered metaphora populace
/tribe depopulated
labyrinthine/
stubborn/
borne of beauty and bullgod gift
spirita people sacrificed ta fulfil destiny/
ta fullfil mythology/
buried in columned obscurity
(bloodred an black security)
hunted by ego *ergo* theseus
/athenian
/purity
rare species of virtual reality/
rare species of virtue / ality

star signa loyalty.

i am *taurus* :
halfman / halfbeast / halftragedy.

i am *modern man:*
a copulatin / decimatin city.

me re-emergence a memory as body of man / head / obscenity
horns **LOCKED**
til the enda tha century.

i am *taurus* /
minos /
mino*taurus* :
KING *bull*,

doan wanna take it *too* seriously).

From
No Mercy

My arms and heart of radius unfixed
    are supple as the swing beam
& whippltree bracket. I am a
    forever busy spur wheel
in the continuous windrow, a
    broadcast distributor of good;
brayed but still unflagged
    beneath plover's wingbeat
& Needle eyes of Light
    your average track-suit city
terrororist is not akin to
    I have soared, peewit-free,
& lived dank in earthe, wormes
    at breastcover, frayed person
with regrets mightily piled,
    autumn seepage rusting
all respected togetherments.
    I have been upright, blade strong,
shattered only in the fastness
    of battle & hearthside
domestic renderings: a soulful
    acolyte certainly
with candle burning, searching
    for a sentence pauseless.

When most commonly employed
    the shin of of my breasts
inverted her pasturage
    in vertical cuts.
I was glorified prince

of beams & Handles.
Tilth turned up
    was of light condition,
for as a child I was raised
    on the wing side,
crested furrows unbroken,
    ridges well set. But
I have my chisel-point,
    when I pulverise & Throw.
I have had my share
    in the breaking of land
& the people on it.
    Short breasts for wide
broken work, breast stays
    not necessary. Then
I am a twisted strap
    lacking simplicity
of fixed wheels, tines
    running but rendered hard
through compression. This
    meant turn-wresting of
intelligence, justice & passion,
    grooves for bolting
to wilderness of Pearl fellsides
    Dark & Steep, for deserting
blood-soaked streets of Albion,
    eased the hammered heart,
as deep frost will cause
    the land to shatter.

Alchemist

my attic full of machinery
like spines of the world
carefully shaped brass
and polished steel
spun as silk

instruments
for exact measurement

city at night
soft metallic moan
short anguished hoot
black river

my beard scorched white
I manufacture ice

clank of iron
on steel track
dogs bark
in a back lane

Razor Job No. 37

There's a monster in the mirror
Mantled in purple midnight
With a cold madness in his eyes

How many lives has he blighted
With his selfish meandering lusts?
How many trusts has he betrayed?

Too many and not enough
To satisfy the aching venom
Of his phoney serpentine rhymes

No love survives long in his
Shrivelled desert of a heart
No religion binds his appetites

Try to touch him: you cannot
Enter his icy glass world
There is no water in his wave

Don't believe the shining razor
He balances on his howling veins
Or any of his hysterical clichés

This monster won't bleed

Portrait of the Writer
as a Young Ass'ole!

In the 'Old Arcade'
a young man
leans casual
against the bar

half pissed
arrogant
hand coils
a tankard

his cigarette
drooping
poseured
on a lip curl

his face
familiar
disturbing

I make to speak

his glance
contemptuous
of age

I move away

and there he is
yesterday
an umbra

gone

only the sneer
an empty glass

nothing
nothing more
remains.

Portrait

Helmet head,
bushy ears,
bobble nose -
ache in tooth just paid for.

Nightie night,
rented bed,
temporary elbow
resting on a Welsh hill.

Line mouth,
shadow eye,
too late night
dark rings of fringe
self cut curl where shouldn't.

Bone face,
neck, chin,
shoulders rounding to a pen,
fingers drawing more lines,
pinched frown.

Tame
someone else's name,
stuck child
talking to her self

portrait.

Gulliver

spread-eagled
shackled at every point
thin wires binding
ground embedded stakes
a circle of pain
each wire tied to an eyelet in his skin
each attempted movement agony

let him twitch a finger
in she jumps
another stake is driven in
his skin is pierced
the eyelet clenched
the wire drawn tight

yet still he smiles
it drives her wild
his body at her whim
his dreams
unfettered
running free

Self-Portrait: *in lieu of a photograph.*

Why should anyone want pictures of poets?

I do not choose to exist as a fixed picture
Inevitably given the lie to later,
Regretted, superseded, taken down
Leaving only a clean patch on the wall.

I should prefer to hang
Not in your mind's gallery but its concert-hall.
I would rather think of you
Taking me home with you, busy in your head.
Playing me daily gaily in the garden,
Humming me happily about your business.

What I am is whatever you see when you hear me.
Whistle me thoughtfully from time to time -
Allegro, ma non troppo vivace.

Refugee

It is not yet over
You have no right to patronise me
You have no privilege to feel my experiences
Fear.
I live in constant fear
I exist in dictatorship and pain.
Memories torture me, control me.
I cannot break free.
Tears against each breath.
Where are my people, my family?
What happened to my land?
My children, my parents, my brothers, my sisters,
Where are you?
I did not cause it. I cannot stop it. Why?
What is this price on my head?
I did not come to beg for survival.
My blood doesn't stop flowing
Though my life is a mosaic of shattered bits.
Keep it together,
Not locked up
In the barracks of amnesia.

He's lain by me all night, that lifetime, that sick
          epoch,
Battered in his vulnerable hours, at the gauntlet's
          other end:

Sometimes his face barred by moonlight sliced
          through stock-car slats;
All laced with phlegm, that sleeping cheek, some
          sulphur-pale, some skimmed in
          plumskin blood.

As long as darkness lasts I lie contorted,
Body half withdrawn to give him room for his repose,
Body half encroaching to protect him from whatever
          threatens yet.
I blow a cooling cone of breath to dry his fever,
Softly draw back saturated hair to clear his brow.

When daybreak unbuttons itself up the east,
When single snub-nosed jumbo-jets come droning in
          on Heathrow, Hamburg, Faro, Leeds,
Starclots of Smarties at their snouts a hundred feet
          above the dipping gulls,
It's time to climb back into that depleted pelt,
Turn the poor sod's ignition and get on with living the
          rest of his life.

A Little Lucky

An old woman stopped my mother on the road to Nine Turns
"Dress her in green," she said, gnarled hand on my head.
"She lucky, dress her in green".

I sit before the mirror, getting ready.
Smoothing moisturiser into my skin,
I touch the mole beneath my left eye
where the cheekbone rises,
and see my brown-skinned cousin in my grandmother's room
push a mole into her chin with a black biro.
"Beauty spot", she told me. "It lucky".

Last time the hairdresser cut my hair
close to the scalp.
Like a cat disturbed in its nap by the fire,
the short perm bristles against my fingers,
then settles with a sigh.
I remove the encroaching albinos from among the black.

Eyebrows are a toddlers squiggles above brown eyes.
Five pounds evened the hills and valleys once.
The sting of protest as each hair was yanked from its mooring,
persuaded me,
the tweezers remain unused in the bathroom cupboard.
The valleys and the mountains have returned.

Lashes are short and curling backwards.
Despite endless coercion, they've never cast
those half-moon shadows on my cheeks.

The lips are a lopsided bow,
the tips point outwards and upwards,
to the place where cheeks are hollow when I smile.
The chin is small,
otherwise unremarkable.

I trawled the children's department
of high street stores to find my size in clothes.
No fat profits from size sixers it seems.
Then someone told me of a petite range somewhere.

I snip the pricey tag from the olive suit,
put it, face up in the drawer as a souvenir.
The price of looking good is steep
when you are short and skinny.

But I wear the curves the cut lends me
like familiar clothes,
draw comfort from the fit,
the adult figure, at last.

Even without the heels
I feel another foot taller,
My daughter peers down at me from her thirteen years.
"What would you like for your birthday, Mum?
A pair of stilts?"

I grow bonsai trees,
Know what it is to look up from a small height,
to shout where others whisper,
To anchor my feet securely
in sifted soil.

There is a circular on the mat.
"This is your lucky day", it says.
The suit rustles as I bend to pick it up.
Is the long wait over then?

Trofannau

Yn y dyddiau cyn bod breuddwydion
Taniwyd yr ynni i'r egin.

A'r plentyn amddifad
Heb neb i'w arwain,
A gafael yn ei law
A Adawyd, a hir oedd ei nos
Heb wawr,
Ei fynwes yn ogof iw ofnau,
A'i ddychymyg byw
Yn gaeth yn ei chôl.

Yn araf
Tyfodd y fflach hen yn olau,
Ynddi 'roedd llawer seren
Llygaid serch a gobaith.
Trwy ddwr a drycin
Cerddwyd lle gynt bu cropian,
Cyn dofi y fflach.
Fel llawer anifail gwyllt.

Ond fyth ymhell
Caed yr hen gysgodion,
Eisteddent ar ei 'sgwyddau
Cydwybod yn amau
Ac yn hollti.
Ar haul melyn a ddygwyd
yn troi a throelli,

Gan glecian yn aur byw
Wrth ei draed
Ei fflamau'n goleuo'i gysgodion
A'i wrechion yn codi,
I'w gadw rhag dig y duwiau.

Rhodd ddirgel y crewr
A llawer cyfrifoldeb cadarn iddi,
Cyn suddo i drwmgwsg
A nodwydd y nos
Yn meddiannu'r breuddwydion,
A'i ddydd yn oeri
A diffodd.

Daeth gwynt y wawr drosto
Gan chwythu'i hanadl oesol
I'r marwor.

Wedi cwsg hir amser
Daeth deffroad
Ac amser i ryfeddu.

Bethan

A glimpse
of distant universe,
a world in dream
beneath the rippled water.
But, drawing near,
water hardens to a mirror,
and there's the familiar shadow
of my own reflection.
Nothing.
but my own reflection.

Bethan

Rhyw gip
ar fydysawd pell,
ar fyd mewn breuddwyd
dan gyffro'r crych.
ond wrth nesáu
caleda'r dŵr yn ddrych,
a dyna gysgod cyfarwydd
fy nelwedd fy hun.
Dim ond
fy nelwedd fy hun.

The Malcontent

I am a malcontent
got every right to be
got no money, got no job
got no property.

I am a malcontent
living in your land
a Marxist revolutionary
a dangerous firebrand.

I am a malcontent
my mind is living free
and you'll never ever stop us
people such as me.

I am a malcontent
an ordinary working man
and I'm gonna blow your arses off
catch me if you can.

chapel

i never wanted to be adorned
i never wished for you to kneel
i never wanted gold
i only wished to inspire
i only wanted a place to believe
i wished for a leak in the roof
to let the rain enter
i never wanted the cut throat
i never wanted assassination
i never wished for flags
i closed my eyes at the marching
i never dreamt of kings
i only hoped for peace
i only wanted prayer
i heard the rain
i felt the wind
i held humanity
i waited in silence
i waited and watched
as the clock changed
i watched as they smashed the windows
stole my treasure
pissed on the floor
and wrote on the wall
i waited and waited as the boards and nails came
i've seen all this before
but the silence held my tongue
the wind wept and the rain ripped
i waited and waited

then, the carpets came
then the cheap objects of desire came
again the place hummed with humanity
people upon their knees   looking for treasure
sounds and time   but then the singing stopped
the faces reddened   the windows darkened
and the   silence   returned;
i waited   i waited
no   body came
the treasure is still here
but now i have my wish,
the roof leaks
i   am not adorned
i   have   no   gold
i have   no   knees
i   am   waiting   wai
ting-

"Wysi(nn)wyg"   Or
What You See Is Not Necessarily What You Get

My hair is going grey and
as usual, I don't know what to do with it.
Cut or grow? Don't know.
I have the usual number of ears,
pointed at the top: pixie's ears, my mother says
(when she's not telling me I'm getting fat).
A nose, of sorts. Blobby. Reacts loudly to Spring.
Just a nose.
My mouth is just a mouth, although prone,
on occasion to breaking out and running off.
The sort of mouth that makes workmen say
"Cheer up, love, it may never happen"
although it usually already has.
My skin more than stretches to cover my face.
It's crumpling a bit with use, and marked
by a full life's laughter.
I look at you from eyes that are
greenish, through lashes
that, without mascara, disappear entirely.

However. Inside my head you may be
startled to know that I am still eighteen.
And in love again, again, again, again.
Inside my head I can sing like Te Kanawa, Pavarotti,
better than the whole Morriston Orpheus Choir.

I can still turn cartwheels, and I slyly peep
from my sparse-lashed, nondescript, greenish eyes
watching young men's rears in tight jeans.

They'd be amazed at what we get up to,
them and me, inside my head.
So when you look at me, remember
What you see is not necessarily
what you get.

Of Myself

How to write
a song of myself?
especialy now
while organising a festival
for Dylan
who seldom wrote
of anything else . . . .

To begin at the
- God no,
who can recall that?
Better
not to begin at all,
let others say or write
what they will - although words
more easily than sticks and stones
can touch that tender spot.

What the hell
I'd still rather not
write my own
epitaph, rather
let anyone at it, even the hacks
- it would have to rhyme, pun, alliterate -
"great guy, had fun,
was always
game for a laugh"

but mark this life somehow
for whatever
the next one lacks.

Self Portrait

There is no romantic setting, but the pose is natural,
a matchstick figure, drawn against an industrial background.

It was easy to draw a face, when I knew nothing of anatomy
and made two black dots for eyes,
a line indicating a nose, too naive to smell out rats,
and a curved mouth, innocent of language.
The adult face,
masked with an undercoat of Pan-stick Fair and Coral Rose,
is more concerned with right angles, a sense of proportion
and a sharper edge to the tongue.

My fingers touch the flat mirror image
but it is difficult to visualise in the round.
I explore the features, and my blind touch reveals
                              the armature of bone,
the planes where skin is stretched to breaking point,
and crevices where anger sometimes lives.

There are two unmatched sides,
but can I show them both at once,
like Picasso's weeping woman?
Draw lashes spread like the feathers
of a cat-mauled crow
and a two-faced grimace poised
on a jagged edge of hysteria?

In a vain attempt, I draw the shaky line
between laughter and tears.

Experience in the life-class dictates a near-sighted view,
but I must look straight in the eye
and it is clear
that the subject is not finished to academy standard.

There is a central light source,
but is it possible to capture spirit with the material?

Oil is not my medium,
for layers take years to harden, and then the knife
                                       can pare away.
Pastels show the softer side, but I need a harder image
to make a point in black or white.

There is need to work quickly in this acrylic age,
No still life here, so I break free,
lose perspective and rule of thumb, in action painting.
Place myself with some abandon,
in the centre of the work,
with slap and drip and dribble,
a little crazing, and a dash of dirty dancing.

Then the happy accident occurs,
and with extravagant gesture,
the cartoon appears,
and I draw in the laughter lines.

Self-Portrait

Mr Spock not the hair the ears
maybe the creases

Ifor nose translated
and the hirsuteness a difficulty
even the voice

LA Law Douglas Brackman and
his half brother reshape the cranium

Worse things tattooed in the
drunken nights out of oil rigs

Smooth Mafioso with shades
observed in supermarkets

On a day of bleak light sometimes
skin crawled with ridges
and the way the mouth hangs

My father the dead man
My fond form
These furrows across my heart
My laughter

Always The Ocean

For those of us born by the ocean
there will always be a listening,
an ear close to the ground
like an animal trailing.

I remember one night
I couldn't see anything of water
and I was sober as the stars,
yet below the tracked paving-stones
and gushing up through cracks.....
benches tilted, clouds rocked.
I was a vessel, filled full of it.

This town at the valley's head
I've adopted or it's adopted me:
wakes fan from the simple phrases
and often laughter can erode
the most resistant expressions.
Despite this, I'm following the river
along our mutual courses:

to the boy on a storm-beach
hopping from boulder to boulder
trying to mimic a mountain-goat;
to the young man sitting in a ring
of perfumed smoke by the castle,
gazing at strings of dolphins
plucked by the slight-fingered sea.

The Museum Piece

Press your face to the showcase,
exhibited, the poet beyond death,
frail for all his strength,
eyeless in submission.

All of a sudden,
words were not enough,
life took him to task.
Finding innocence refused
        on the infant fingerprint,
He tumbled wildly
        on the litter wind.
Blind as an alley,
wingless onto the scrabbled bed
that nailed the child in him.

An improbable saviour even now,
'Pinned-on-card' beauty
        dead as bones under museum lights,
No mourners here
        just tourists and flies.

Five Faces

In response to the photograph "Herod, 1993"
by the Czech surrealist artist Roman Kubik.

The original family tree
interned in its own bark,

lips sealed tight against
the slowest executioners -

dark-hooded clouds that wield
the wind's persistent axe,

rainsnipe and sunblast,
poultices of snow that decompose....

heads bowed,
cheek to cheek in prayer

for the ivy that lives
on every victim's corpse

and yet must still aspire
to some notion of heaven.

Naked Playing The Cello

Bristols Bristols Crescendo!
Long-necked like a woman
mirrored-up with a certain smile.

Right nipple glances outward
Bellows bowing arm reveals
hides
black pit mouth hair.

Hard cello
press
Cold cello
Chair buttock-spread.

Moisture gulps out
will it all fall away!

With friction wood warms
shadow
cello pressures leg
pinching pinching suede knees.

Upwards
gentle gradient of flesh curves
hip-nobble smoothed over
continuum
pale wing pulls and closes.

Side view:
perfect snail shell scroll
thick ponytail gleaming
light

round brown mark on haired white thigh
shoulder
cream

as vibrations chase through horse hair
string
in wood
radiate in hidden left breast
deep notes are the best.

Corset-waist cello
striped
carved
twiddled
is played.

Time-lapse photography
like the decaying mouse
speeds bowing
a sawing mad cacophony
whirr of demented spider left
begins to fail
body round the cello shrivels
crisp packet in fire.

Spectrum sound narrows
becomes a reed
churning light catches wood-grain cello
just the same
gleams on varnish,
rattles lost in her maze of grey.

Four Studies: Configuring Love
(pour ma belle de la gare)

1.

Until I was twenty-nine years old, I thought silence was
the language of Love.

               At thirty, I thought it was Hungarian
and ardently pursued the tongue of the Magyar (for the
better part of three months, at least).

                       At forty-one, the
language of Love seems something evolving in the future of
the species. All humans and their sounds being heirs to
a marvel not yet born.

                 The sound of Love will be a par-
lance like no other in existence. By passing both lips and
mind, it will enter the heart like the singing of Seraphim.

Like Esperanto, it will be understood all around the world:

unlike Esperanto, it will not sound like lobsters fucking
in the bottom of an old metal dory.

delirio

madreselva primavera telaraña naranjal

ruiseñores azahares mariposa carnaval

aguileña rociada giaconda perejil

mariquita pequeñita esmeralda luz frágil

alborda graciosa melodía lirio

flauta dulce campanilla besos de delirio

cinta seda cima copa luna llena turpial

prado verde chiquitina riachuelo manantial

agua pura cristalina manzanilla pasión

ojos claros amorosos garza sueño ficción

añoranza sonatina zarzuela mirabel

arco iris amarilis uva lira sol miel

efímero espejo promesas de la vida

tapiz de mi corazón quimera ensartada

The Last Night Of The Year:
Elegy For Harri Webb (Died 31.12.94)

When I came home after four months away
Everything had changed. My daughter's hair
Was a shaggy gold over her black scarf
And there was a ruby in her ear:

On the house the roof was gone, the old
Bethesda slates with their edges crumbling
Into cigarette ash had been replaced
By wet-look tiles, so now there are no

Original buildings left in our street.
Under the roof where once the attic lay -
That stifling chamber where the cistern hissed
And a locked suitcase that one day

I had promised to force, grew coarse
With slatedust - there was a new room, pillared
With sunshine that came in through a skylight.
That last night I stood under its cold

Triptych of glass and saw the new-born blue
Of Sirius, the emaciated moon
Over Cog-y-Brain where the first people
Of this country had lived amongst limestone,

Lighting their fires, speaking an unknown
Language, camped like the tribes of bikers
And lepidopterists who crouch there yet,
Stirring the embers, simple and absolved.

And pressing closer I felt the frost
Like a bruise and saw beyond the duneland
The pit of the ocean that terrifies,
And then a silhouette of England,

Black Exmoor, so much wilder than we think.
Below me, all the revelry was stilled
For the second of midnight. A complete silence.
In our own ways we saw the old year killed.

Snapshots

Catch this
in one instant
isolated in time
as like to sketch
an English garden
through all its years
and seasons
in a single frame

•

Drawing Breath

Hooked on their long notched legs
They stand on these bouncing panicles.

Within the shifting glow
the faceted mounds of their eyes,
I must be recorded, a safe
unimportant stillness in this angled
opening and closing of wings.

Edges of shade, self cast,
interrupt the sun, triangles
of beating, unsteady darkness.
When they fall wide open,
a dying light catches
in the mammoth-red of their fur.

A summer wind from the east
ruffles it with hints of ice.

Glaciers. They were once here,
pressing, releasing the land
through the short pulse of our time.
A wave travelling beneath us,
is dropping the crust to the sea.
Where a new ice age may meet it.

The buddleia's weighty sprays
seem to draw breath. Nuptial
butterflies tumble among swallows,
wobble down to feed. One is wafted,
rustling, to the page, tests it.
Her trunk is a hair-spring
uncoiling, tasting the whiteness.

She has reached the end of her changes.

But as she explores these pits,
these bumps, the residue of trees,
I glimpse her descendants, sucking
traces from the face of ice-floes,
finding cracks of climate to weld
their tight-ribbed eggs to.

Thorns To My Right

Clinging to the makeshift precipice
I chose the easy way
and swung to the left

I now border
between negative solutions

But I don't need patience here
just the stamina
to bare the sluggish rhyme

and even though the pit deepens
my conceptions grow taller

Still Life

There is nothing like this
paint, loaded brush
sized canvas, empty house

Still life of cream lace
white bowl, two duck eggs
and a vase of Iceberg roses

It's not silent, cars come and go
wood pigeons sound like kids
practising recorders in the park
stray voices lose themselves
up and down the hill

But it feels silent because I'm still
I can hear myself breathe
I can hear hog hair scumble Irish linen
and the gargling whirlpool in the jam jar
as my brush turns water titanium white

I dip into a wet spiral of leaf green
search out subtle tones
licks of shadow
startling stars of light
suggestions of blue and yellow
appear in eggshell more delicate
than best china cups

A bug crawls across a petal-falls
paddles air before righting itself
The telephone rings

realise the children will
be home from school

house a shambles
beds unmade and nothing
for tea but duck eggs

and a beautifully laid table
roses, just for you, I'll say
cleverly nipping complaints
inside tight little buds.

"I Am What Is Around Me"
(Wallace Stevens)

These then make a portrait;

high-walled garden,
birds in plenty,
noisy she-dog,
lone live toad

& more indoors;
ceramic tortoise,
flying horse
a wingless dragon.

"These are merely instances."

Cracking Up

It doesn't really suit me, I thought,
surrounded by pouting, moulded females.
In the gloss of their skin
I saw me reflected as a pockmark,
me as a mistake.

"It's just not like you," he said
when I tried to bake cakes, iron collars, de-flea and
de-mould.
"You're wild, impulsive!"
"Creative abandon won't get the curry stain out of the
carpet,"
                                        I thought.

I'm not that kind of daughter
I pondered, choosing a card,
there were bunnies and bouquets in abundance.
My love's real, not printed,
but one more pert kitten won't kill me , will it?

At each turn
a facet,
my face should fracture
under the pressure.

The Watcher

I am the watcher.
The one who walks away
And waits, silent and alone.
Observer of brown birds,
small, by hidden streams.
Namer of undistinguished weeds
In corners of forgotten fields.
Plodder in the undergrowth,
Loiterer in the thicket,
Ready to call all to mind,
Find the new, classify the old,
Recognise the different,
Pleasure in the indifferent.
You may call me loner,
And say that I disdain
The sanctity of human kind,
But walk with me on any woodland path
And I will show you things
You never knew existed,
Things you cannot even see,
To fatten out your shallow days

50-Word autobiographies

1

White-grey skies then & quickening clouds through
glass • white breathlessness • houses • then spread I
too big for the house & the white-blue street

into comradeship then • & the world cracked wide •
the wrestle for sex • then the West & the West then
• some years of gathering, certain joy

*

2

From a hill-top sun & wind I travel back
   to warehouses -
      silence & sun on a steelworks wall
   some fog
     streets
       some buses

back -
before
before my birth
   no snap
     I've walked this way to

Twyn-y-Gaer,
     in sun
  & wind
     and I am 45

*

3

Across the road was a path to the endless fields -

My mother's box - it was bakelite brown, & in it an
autograph book with pink & yellow perfumed pages

My father's shed - my ray-guns, red & green & yellow
beams - woodsmell & creosote

Sunday radio music

   the lyrics \
     all the time

*

Dealing From The Hand

Lived abroad,
Learned a bit,
Been thin and fat;
Done all that.

Skin sagging in places;
Won't say where.
Lines are carved now
Deeper than smile creases.
They don't go away.

Hair's abandoing ship;
Clings around the rafts
Of plug hole and pillow.
On board, the grey invaders
Will soon be winning
Against what's left.

Once played
Football, cricket, even rugby
After a fashion.

Found that inside us
Is the horizon
That matters;
Still trying to find
And share it.

Four kids sleeping upstairs
Leech money, time and love,
Nearly everything I have.
They're welcome.

One knuckle's humped to a ridge
From not catching that ball
In the nets.

This gold ring
Grips another finger tight,
Holds our lives together.

Exhumed centuries hence,
A few stray bones turned over
By some synthetic metal plough,
They might notice this worn groove
Above the joint

And wonder, like me,
What it all means.

FRANCESCA.
I just keep smiling
well past the point of no return.

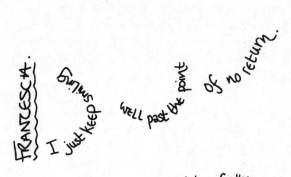
← rub here for the
calming and illusory
scent of lavender.

Moore
Recumbent Figure, 1934

unnh   grunnh?   grohh
wassamatter? Wh'am I? Who the ? No
go'way. I was dreaming. I was deep.
Where was I? Dancing. Arm in arm in . . .*She*.
All round me. We were waltzing, slow
slow, round and round. And suddenly
there's all this . . . *unstuff*. Is it sky?
I never asked. You did this to me
damn you. You made me this: I

am. But I can take it. Mass-
culine, I ham, a bullwork. Charlie Atlas
torse, the strangth of clunched hands,
nubbled biceps (feel that!) in a man-
to-manly buddy-hug.
                              But mateless,
muzzlebound, manhandling . . .
unthings. Unnh. A not-
hole in the heart. *You*, you abandoned
me, you left me wanting . . . what?

The words gro wrong. It's a terribore
think, this onliness, this wanting . . . *more*.
There must be others, no? No eyes to see,
I not-quite-touch them, close. Quick flimsy
curious things, warm breaths.
                              I'm floored,
yes down but no not out - a lourdly
drunk who might yet lurge upright, embrace
the emptiness and astonish the dance-floor
with a coup of (how to put it?) grace.

Saturday

Going to the bookstall
know it is Saturday
after Friday night with friends
                trading
sparks of conversation
          a suitcase of experience
      a kiss
to twinkle darkness
         like wonder
I am my own child playing
        imagination's detritus
speaking first important words
         & hearing
a language   inanimate things
       the sentiment of rocks
          replacing taint
    a paint-flaked wall

Going to the bookstall
know it is Saturday
       unlocking night
        each different key
enjoying   music of argument
       conflict's symphony
        wind & tree
      rain & roof
     unsheltered
I have Tarzan's belief
     his primitive call
        BEAUTIFUL
Saturday at the bookstall

Grandfathers, Grandmothers

Warwickshire bred us, mother, daughter,
father and further back long dead grandfather,

proudly his own man delivering coals
on his back as merchant sprung from pitman boy

entering the Griffe Colliery at 11
and by 21 out, never spoken of again.

Warning his son: *Get a trade* to live, for respect,
fear-driven, the need to rise above his station.

My father into the factory at 14, toolmaker
apprentice, nightschool with his bible:

The Mechanic's Handbook with its thumbnail index,
everything in there gold text, somehow the answer

to everything. And grandmother small and old
in the Home for Incurables. The long boredom

filled Sunday visits, asked to play in the gardens
outside and then brought to her briefly

like a presentation at Court, hand trembling
bedridden, taking tea from a spouted cup,

hardly known as I kept my well behaved place
and never spoke until spoken to. My allegiance

to my mother's mother, the true matriarch,
thrice-married with a bevy of children

all dotted around Warwickshire - aunts and
one uncle who was in disgrace - Ida who had loved

not wisely but well, on her own and working
as canteen manageress among the big steel pans

and smells in Birmingham's great firm,
Stewart & Lloyds, maker of tubes, all sizes,

and so the story goes: it was sent one day
the smallest tube in the world by a rival

in America - and returned the tube with a tube
inside. Grandfather Clem, deserted for a roving

sea-captain, was the weak one, who at 21
had his proud debut as a solo pianist at

Birmingham Town Hall, and then was stricken
by sleeping sickness. His palsied hands only

fit for serving in his family draper's shop
and for teaching piano to cane rapped children.

I remember his dogs, Alsatians kept in sheds,
and his second marriage idiot child, the punishment

not wished on wicked Auntie, stepmother
to my mother and left behind sister and brother.

The Witch who never let my mother clean her teeth
who cut off her red curls, who tried to make plain

her beauty, who punished and overpunished
with deprivations and Puritan hatred,

who called the missing Ida: *The Scarlet Woman*.
Who my mother met secretly outside school

and when at last the schoolgirl went to work,
she ran away to *Her* and returned triumphant,

first pay packet all spent on a bright red
lipstick, high heels and cherry bobbing hat.

Portrait Of The Artist

Four faces, but this is the one I've chosen:
a young Renaissance man
painted into a small square frame

because of the clever gleam
of humour touched in
dark eyes that follow you round the room.

An heirloom from a distant benefactor:
a gift, or a lengthy loan,
this portrait that hangs on my dream

wall in my house of sleep, a keepsake
looking out from a shadowed space
with his neat trimmed beard

and a rim of lace at his neck,
his curls a little tousled as befits
an artist, as he lightly regards himself

in an unseen mirror, also regarding me
from the place where my mirror ought to be.
Is he an ancestor, or a lost cousin?

We share a dusky look, though my hair
hangs loose, and my tits are fuller.
But scrape at the painted layers, and see

what's hidden under the brushwork -
the sketches, the drafted faces may appear
and the blood lines, and the ancestral places:

arched Norfolk brows and the tip-tilted nose,
Saracen eyes from Spain
from Gwent the lips' plump curve,

cheekbones looted from the New World
with the mouth-jut, the scant chin -
and from the Clwydian hills, my skin, my name.

Now I recognise him for what I am -
we're painted in together:
he is my other self, my night brother

my co-conspirator, my vanity
made visible, my heart, my poetry -
my given, finished picture.

Self Portrait

Face a red planet
smudged by glasses, he's
slumped in the bus seat

As the sun rises, illuminating
the little bits of whisker
he's missed, iron filings

On the nodding red planet.
How small his hands are.
How Elvis his hair is.

He may be a collapsing balloon,
chins folded like dough,
sun reflects on the glasses.

Off The Wall

I would have been a signed masterpiece
But there were always   mind police
I grew up with them

Poets
Lovers
Revolutionaries
Zen
& God   amen

All together in their wails

Ponty boys rule O.K.   Ray's Gay
Dai ♥ K
Axe poll tax

                                 Kil Gang

Christ saves   All
At   Gateways
Wall

i

i am infant
freeing me
from mother

a mouth chew
-ing words
into speech   i am the first day at school

i am child   **shot tall**
          shooting ball
sounding **loud** against the disused fence

          proud youth   playing with pimples
          exploring growth   between silent sheets

i am stranded in the pub's back room
underage
"an Oi boy"   with untrained hands

fumbling lines in my Ben Sherman shirt
          until   like a difficult button
               i get lucky
                    there **&** then   think **i'm** man   until
                         finally   filling pews   taking vows
                         building dreams in a daisy world
                    i become family

               complex \ simple   one divine unit

designed for separation
                              or am i

or is it   society

      bonding the weak to strong ideas
      brazing nations in the heat of battle
           where dead men

owned a flat

        world

for a while   **i am content**

  bumping and grinding in real time   in

shifting allegiance like plates at a buffet

a world

of fragile importance

where rock and life - are linked - and spin

a universe   of splinters

caught in the sound of a fucking big ban**g**

zer°

      i am the whole of creation
       pulled from the womb
        and sucking
       on my mother's breast

        my hand begins
       by clutching space

        i am the eyes
         in the face
      of that new born
          child

     shut tight against the light

       or am i

Latest Publications

Tilt.   *Hartill \ Hool \ Jones.*
                  ISBN 1 899449 30 2
                  £5.95

Of Sawn Grain.   *Edited by Anne Cluysenaar.*
                  ISBN 1 899449 35 3
                  £5.00

Making It.   Ric Hool
                  ISBN 1 899449 45 0
                  £5.95

More titles available on request

How You Can Help

You can support The Collective by ordering any of
the above from your local bookshop or direct from
the address on the facing page. The money raised
goes back into publishing poetry, supporting poets
both new and established.   You can further
support poetry through subscription to poetry
magazines and by attending poetry readings at
venues throughout the UK. Look out for Collective
run events or, if you would like one in your area,
get in touch with the Co-ordinator, address as
before.

About # The Collective

e-mail   john.jones6@which.net

The Collective is a non-profit-making organisation formed in 1990 to promote and publish contemporary poetry. Funds are raised through a series of poetry events held in and around South Wales, mainly the Abergavenny area. Many major poets have read for the organisation and been strongly supported by *'new writers'* from Wales and farther afield. The backing and generosity of fellow writers is a cornerstone of The Collective's success. Vital funding comes from public bodies including the Arts Council of Wales and donations are often received in support of the movement from members of the public. If you would like to find out more about The Collective and its work then contact:

The Co-ordinator
The Collective
Penlanlas Farm
Llantilio Pertholey
Y-Fenni
Gwent
NP7 7HN
Cymru
U.K.

fish